Twist of Love

A selection of poems

by

Rosemary May Wells

Foreword

There are times when we look back on life and think
How did I ever do that? I feel that about most of these
poems, nearly all of which were written 15 to 20 years
ago. We go through different stages in life and lockdown
in 2020 created a watershed from which to look back,
hence the first section: Stages of life. It also gave time
to reflect and focus on what one truly loves and that
fell naturally into friends, places and the natural world.
Certain events are of global significance and often
spark thoughts and responses heard in conversation.
And Reflections express universal themes that we all
experience. From time to time I touch down with
humour and the absurd – a necessary ingredient to the
happy life.

I offer this second volume of poems with gratitude
for all those who have enriched my path in life.

Rosemary Wells
January 2022

To Annie

She tapped a spring
and the door flew open.
For years I had lain hidden
quiet within me
happy to act on the edge
at the back of other peoples lives
but aware of the gallon within me
trickling out through the pint pot.
But she tapped a spring.
Suddenly a way opened.
My gallon went whoosh –
and has never ceased to flow.

With grateful thanks to Sue Wheeler
for her original cover design –
and to David Mason
for his patient technical help.

Contents

Section One

Stages of Life

Section One

Stages of Life

The Passionate Pilgrim

Response to The Passionate Pilgrim – Shakespeare

Crabbed age and youth should live together
Youth is full of risk, age is full of wisdom;
Youth like spring vitality, age like autumn colour;
Youth like summer joyance, age like winter valour;
Youth is full of energy, age's breath is slow and sure;
Youth is agile, age is sprightly.
Youth is heedless, age attends more.
Youth is foolish, age is learned.
Age, I do salute thee
Youth, I do refute thee.
Oh, my love, my love is learned.
Age is comfort, wisdom garnered.
Hie thee hither, stay a-while,
Do not enter thou denial.
Breathe the fruits of life's immensity
Shepherd, protect from youth's intensity.
Youth's a song, yet to be sung.
Join age's rich voiced harmony.

Free

Footloose and fancy free
the baby
crooked in the security
of its mother's arm
flailed its feet about
unshod
looking around
unquestioningly
in contented observation.
No imagined fancies
To fear its being;
its mind as unfettered
as the freedom
of its curled toes.

Offering

Consider a child's painting:
By most objective standards, it is not good art,
but when placed proudly in the parents hands
it has tremendous worth, delighting the heart,
if not always the eye.
Gentle questioning will be required
to establish what the picture represents,
and which way up it should be hung.
The answers will become part of the wonder,
recalled each time the adult eye lingers
over the work,
now mounted on some kitchen cupboard,
or fridge door.
In the moment of giving and receiving,
which is the lover, which the beloved ?
The child's glad offering
and the adult's glad receiving
are each their own counterpart,
in a story of love,
given and received, received and given.

Trust Life

Trust life –
My Quaker friend more than advised –
Trust life – with a strength
that penetrated my consciousness.
I thought of parents who are meant to know best.
And education that got you where you were meant to be
and God who had something to do with it all.
Trust life.

And now, – a lifetime on, – I think again :
Trust life –
And how life varies so,
for some the luck, for some the loss.
And how fulfilment changes with the passing years,
and what we thought should be has passed us by.
And yet, and yet,
not what life does for us so much
as what we give to life has seen us through.
And yet,
that unexpected element that rises up
and touches us with blessing
and with hope.
Trust life – and we are part of of life –
Trust love.

Crossing to the Isle of Wight

The wake of my life
trails out behind me
lit by sunshine.
Ahead, the masts of many boats
beckon, glowing
as a cloud of light,
until nearness distinguishes
individuality.
From the mid-point,
looking behind and before,
the past merges
into a continuing stream,
rippling with little undercurrents.
The future separates out
with nearness – each mast
a journey to be taken,
for pleasure or for work.
At the mid-point
there is poise.

Middle Age

If anyone had told me
when I was young and carefree
I would spend my middle years
shopping and washing up –
I would not have believed them.
I would have said –
Life is for more than that.
Life is for putting the world to rights.
Life is for changing the world for the the better.
Life is to pursue an ideal,
to follow aspirations,
to add a little uniqueness,
a little greatness, perhaps, to life.
Life is not for shopping and washing up.

But now as I shop for the elderly friend
who cannot go out –
choosing especially her favourite things –
knowing I am the person in her life
who makes her a person too
rather than just a hapless recipient
of well-meaning, if necessary, care;
and as I wash up for the friend
whose kitchen is indescribable,
and yet I look out on her garden and see
an early brood of starlings –
I think, this is life –
not to change the world,
but to relieve the lives of individuals –
each life a world in itself –
and so create a happiness.

Outside – Inside

You see
old people struggling with their sticks
struggling to get about with their difficulties.
I see
friends, with long personal histories
and interesting lives.

You see
a Meeting on the edge of survival
and anxious concern about the future.
I see
a still centre in the Meeting for Worship,
a quiet confidence radiating from inner strength.

You see
people whose values were formed so long ago –
how relevant could they be today?
I see
Friends, whose lives have been fashioned
out of hard-won experience –
whose values the world today needs.

You see
the coming to an end of what once
might have been vital living.
I see
continuing life, love and laughter,
lived to the last drop of life
squeezed from the limiting body.

You see
a need that could be burdensome
I see
a loving delight to do what one can.

Looking Back

Look back on life, the mountains and the molehills,
the ragged edges of life's uncertain path,
the twisted threads of darkness and redeeming,
the play of light and shadow through the years.

Look back on life, the compassion and forgiving
of younger self that strove too hard for life;
the golden thread of love that wove a pattern
and faith that gave the strength to live, endure.

Look back on life, the unexpected flowering;
mistakes that yielded wild flowers by the way;
the certainties that blinded us to gifts
and hidden strengths and graces others gave.

Look back on life, the hope that ever lingered
round edges of disaster and despair,
that out of tragedy may spring the seeds of love
and laughter; the joys of small deeds shared and won.

Look back on life, and life's unanswered questions
that hover still at some deep level of the mind, but
see the love grown through the turmoil and contentment;
give thanks that love is still the answer we must find.

Section Two

The Natural World

Section Two

The Natural World

Alone in a bluebell wood

The bluebells are silent under the canopy
of birdsong.
Only the pervasive blueness draws attention,
as far as the eye can see –
sprinkled with the stars
of wood anemones.
A green woodpecker throws its yaffling cry
across the glade.
A pair of ducks raise questioning heads
above the height of grass
around the puddles.
A world silent, yet song full –
a secret world
only I know.

The Lime Tree

The grains of the bark
ran up the trunk
like water circumnavigating
a pebble, surrounding
the faults, the bulges,
creating patterns
of beauty, out of
variation.

Thus a sculptor
works the knot
into a conspicuous place,
creating beauty out of
awkwardness.

Tree, water, sculptor,
each according to their nature
overcome obstacles,
attain their end,
beauty.

Daffodils

I am a rescuer of fallen daffodils.
The glade where ducks,
web-footed, wander between
clumps of two-tone trumpets,
was scattered with bent fronds,
windblown
and vandal switched.
The heads lay apart,
snapped off; yet still their glory
outshone lost dignity.
Some I restored,
lifting their heads, weatherbeaten
to the shame of level earth,
again to spring and duck
to the wind's play.
Others I gathered,
bounty of a dawn morning,
to beautify my home,
tall and broken, short and bent,
limp and insect bitten.
Like humans, various
in their quality,
yet, lovingly tended,
glorifying their kind.

Rain

A benison of the earth is rain.
To wake in the early hours
hearing the steady downpour of rain
watering the earth,
is to lie, listening, listening
as the earth receives its deep
penetrating gift,
to recall childhood memories
of sitting by a window, watching
as the hours go by,
the steady downpour of West Country rain.
Not for England hot, dusty days,
but rather warm moistness,
with umbrellas and wellies and
splashing in puddles. Revelling
in the wetness of things.

Incident at Ballard Lake

The randy Canada goose
honked its pursuit
of a not-to-be-won-over female,
rebutted with a mere
beakful of feathers.
The female strutted off,
its dignity almost unruffled.
The male, undeterred,
not stopping in flight, alighted
on a second, equally unco-operative female.
The third obliged.

Snail Love

Two snails emerged from the watercan,
as I filled it at the butt,
disturbed by the thundering cascade.
Balanced on the precarious edge
they climbed around each other
neck over shell,
waving their antennae –
for comfort in the face of danger threatened ?
or for love discovered in a watery pledge ?

Cyclamen

Like butterflies tethered
unwillingly to earth
the cyclamen petals stretch upwards
on their long stems,
poised, as if to take flight.

Tomatoes

This year is the Year of Tomatoes.
Last year was the Year of Apples.
And the year before the Year of Plums.
But this year is the Year of Tomatoes.
Home-grown, small, sweet and juicy,
so abundant on the stem,
they need to be picked off delicately
when ready to fall.

I shall remember the year of tomatoes,
watching, like traffic lights,
the green turning to red –
Stop – in your tracks –
Eat and enjoy.

Bracken

The herald of tree turning
is the bracken, bronzed
in the sunlight, like an Attic shield,
harbinger of autumn.
The trees turn slowly,
yet suddenly have arrived
in flame-gold, flame-orange, flame-red,
Still, utterly still,
poised,
waiting in glory
for the unseen force to come
and wrestle with its fragile hold
and lay its glory at our feet –
to be scuffed along,
trampled through,
and trod with plodding pleasure
by kids and grown up children.

The bracken stays,
yielding its depth of sunlit bronze
gradually
to the muted tones of winter.
It, too, had its glory in the fall.

Cock crow to Owl hoot

From cock-crow to owl hoot
the old saying
lingers on only in classics,
whose authors know the intimate connection
between language and natural life.

Cock-crow startles the morning air –
alerting living things to wake
to be aware.
Townees complain, who
sans a murmur
ignore an urban traffics roar.

Owl hoot catches the wandering ear –
a whiff of country
in the density of town –
evoking loneliness
and presence.

Section Three

Friends

Section Three

Friends

Pat

She was fun and she was thankful.
These were the twin poles of her existence.
The children loved her for it.
To be taken out of class
for reading to Mrs Bradford
was a treat.
Her husband, no doubt, loved her for it
when his wheelchair pulled along her roller skating
in one glorious rush of speed.
And at the Rest Home, all she could say was:
'I'm so thankful,' over and over.
And she would add:
'I'm so lucky, and what is more,
I know it.
Other people are lucky but they don't know it
so they miss out.
But I know it.'

For Penny

Never mind 'Queen of the fairies' –
She was Queen of her friends
the day we sat down to celebrate
with wine, quiche and scrumptious salad
the birthday not to be named.
Conversation flowed by candlelight,
ranging over life, morality and ghosts.
An artist sketched; and gradually
spirits lifted as each gave something
unique to the whole. Links forged,
Strangers met as friends, and presiding –
one whose gift for friendship brought us all together.

Peter

He lived his life
a raw deal –
with humour, sanguine philosophy,
and a gift for friendship,
also generosity.
'Well, what can you do' he would say
When yet another person benefitted
from his open-handedness.
Wherever he went he made friends,
in the church, at work,
in hospital, at the Day Centre.
So across the social board
his friends respected him,
benefitted from and were strengthened
by his capacity to keep going.
Sometimes he'd flip,
shout down the phone:
'I don't want to see you again, that's it.'
But he always came round –
anxious he'd said nothing
to hurt or upset.
Marriage would have made him.
A physical kind of chap, it would have fulfilled him.
But he believed it wrong to pass on his illness
to the next generation,
and could he have withstood the tensions ?
He took pleasure in simple things;
a game of scrabble, chess (especially to win!),
films, his books, sport on television.

In a quiet way
He had gained much philosophy about life.
'You mean a lot to many people, Peter,' I said to him.
'I know,' he said, with quiet assurance.
Underneath it all, his faith as a Christian
was a particular commitment
given he was a Jew by birth.
A life, fulfilled inwardly
and faithfully lived.

Sister Elizabeth Julian

Poise, quiet presence
and a light sense of humour
characterised this most special
of Sisters.
Alongside the strict discipline of her life
lurked a zest for living,
a desire to know, to understand,
and not to miss
any new experience or piece of knowledge.
So grew her wisdom –
that quiet composure and perception
that weighed and considered,
then said just the right word
to make you feel understood,
cared for.
Never any attention to herself
but a light humour deflecting it away
and drawing you into the centre
of her loving concern.

How many lives were touched
by her calm spirit, her joy in living.

Win

'Stand up, stand up' she commanded with laughter.
She looked down at her ancient boobs,
As if, even in this moment of extreme distress,
picked up from her fall on the floor,
she was inwardly still a young girl,
full of youthful vitality and life.
'Don't tell my daughters,' she pleaded,
'Don't tell my daughters.' I knew then
she cherished independence more than health,
more than life itself.

Luke

He sat on a chair in the centre of us all,
a little ungainly in his near manhood,
a little awkward with his partially controlled limbs,
while we danced around him
an ancient Aramaic prayer song,
swinging to and fro,
head dipping, lightness of step,
as we called on the mind to enter the heart
and express light and peace.

Sometimes he joined in
With a sure sense of rhythm,
Swaying to and fro,
wholly secure in the knowledge
of being loved.
Cuddles, chat and caress followed.
A focus of love and attention –
and out-flowing peace.

Anne

In the further reaches of dementia
her love of words and imagination
never entirely left her.
Struggling with a covered cup of milk –
which way to turn its 'snout'
as she called it,
and a biscuit – which to take first?
"This needs de-awkwardising" she said.

Section Four

Loved Places

Section Four

Loved Places

Tanners Lane

Between high tide and low tide choose
low tide.
High tide laps, storms, waves,
its fullness buoyant but unchanging.
Low tide murmurs,
creeping streamlets over mud and mossy swards,
curlews unfolding cry,
cheep and chirrup of unknown birds
as they settle for the night.
Even the skies seem to murmur
as cirrus and cumulus merge
into the darkness of night.
Quiet activity of a subdued landscape
forever changing.
Muted colours blended between
Moss green, mud browns, seagull white
and sparkling reflection of sky-y light

Choose low tide for stillness, awareness,
shimmering aliveness.

Lymington Quay

Grey masts
against a greying sky.
Majesty.
Mooring of boats,
colourful, and upturned
against dimming light on the water.

A seagull swoops
to meet its shadow
touches down
and is off.

Ducks trail the water
breaking reflective lines of colour
with their wake.

On shore, here, there,
stand lone individuals
held by the solemnity
of greying masts
against a dimming sky.

Mottisfont

Riot of roses,
foiled by the foxgloves
that fling their sprays towards
the fragrant climbers.
Old roses here, from many centuries,
even 'Ancient' ones,
halfway between the natural dog-roses
and modern blooms –
red and white streaked,
scent, softly sifting on the breezy air,
all burgeoning among country garden flowers,
like Canterbury bells, love-in-the-mist....

No formal garden this
of neatly thought out plan.
Only a reticent eye
behind the intermingling
of rosy rarities and common garden flowers,
contained within the warmth
of tall red walls.

Seclusion here, containing
one man's dream to harvest roses
from the earliest times.
Flowered history, caught
in scent and colour.

Portesham, the Old Vicarage

I open my window.
A rose reaches up to me –
one sweet scent
from a plethora, climbing
up the old stone house –
valerian and roses in season
entwining
into the caught crevice,
the walls asking to be hidden
secreting the knowledge of years.
Has there always been calm
in this still house ?
Or is the calm the gift
of the stones that endure
after the transient busy-ness of human living
has passed.

The stones are silent.
So is the rose,
but it gives to me its sweetness.

St. Mary Magdalene cemetery

I love the unkempt beauty
of this quiet corner –
God's little acre –
especially Spring harvest time
when crocuses, windblown
this way and that
mingle their mauves and white
amidst the uneven grass
with scattered clumps
of fragrant primroses.
The 'little humble celandine'
holds its own too,
Its velvet yellow out-shining
windswept daffodils.
Here squirrels play.
To watch their flight
from branch to branch
chasing each other
through the tangled mess
of overhanging foliage
is to glimpse
playfulness
at the heart of all things,
to perceive joy
in the carefree abundance
of Creation.

Section Five

Happenings

Section Five

Happenings

The Millennium Bug

The Millennium Bug
Exploded –
and
The trains didn't run
Buses ground to a halt
The cars wouldn't start
The computers said 'Shan't'
and yes,
Water didn't flow in the taps
The heat turned off
Cookers did go cold.
But for one glorious moment
The world was
STILL.
Then God relented.
'Have it your own way'
he said.
And with a burring and a whirring
A hooting and a pooping
A rushing and pushing
A buzzing and fussing
We
Shot into the 21st century.

Iraq – March 2003

They have bombed the heart out of Iraq –
a heart already dark
with many evil deeds.
The thin membrane of normal life
is punctured.
A black hole appears,
out of which, mindless, uncontrolled acts of darkness
spew.

Revenge, an arrogant sense of mission,
and illegality,
has done this.
Weep, weep for those who pay
double
for the sins of others.

Continental Drift

The plates are always on the move
bump into each other.
A bit broken off here.
A mountain ridge reared up there.
Imperceptibly
the Earth shifts.

People are on the move.
Not the quiet going about one's business movement,
the necessary journey from here to there.
But the drifting of masses to and fro,
from east to west, west to east,
the pleasure industry gone mad.
There is more on the other side of the world,
more life, more interest, more experience.
More, more, more.
Be on the move and you're living.

There is a dark side.
People fleeing from fear,
terror in their homeland,
moving away, away, away.
Be on the move and there is hope.
Maybe.

Continental drift.
The earth shifts.
It too has its dark side,
Volcanoes erupt, landslides, earthquakes.
But at least the Earth rests,
lies dormant in the in between times.

But will the people ever rest ?

Pre-Coronavirus – 2018

For the ancient Egyptians
The slow cycle of time was measured
in millennia.
In the West, the turning centuries
marked the passage of time.
In the twentieth century, each decade
had its own characteristic.
In the twenty-first century –
who would have guessed five years ago
the all-pervading influence of the internet –
And who can imagine five years hence ?

When will the spinning top of the world
topple over ?

Response – 2020

The world did not topple over –
It was made to stop in its tracks.
Interconnectedness has its drawbacks.
To fly globally has its excitement.
To holiday abroad broadens the mind,
can create a sense of shared humanity.
To trade globally offers endless variety.
But the virus can fly globally too –
on the backs of people
perpetually on the move.
An invisible break
on the spinning top of the world.

Did I ever imagine?

Did I ever imagine
that at 74 years old –
if I ever speculated about such an exalted age –
I would be lying out in the grass
looking up at the deep blue of the sky
through the sunlit blossom of the blackthorn tree
watching the wisps of cloud drifting along
in the light breeze,
as I used to do as a child ?
As I loved to do as a child ?

The world has gone mad with rush and restlessness,
and I caught up in it,
fitting things in, taking little heed,
as life flitted by.
I almost envied those who were 'laid aside'.
But now we are brought to a standstill,
forced to limit our lives,
to accept boundaries
we thought we had broken for all time.
Leaving only the essentials of life –
Being, rather than doing,
reciprocal care, inner resource,
and appreciation of life itself.

Covid

The world is suddenly silent.
What do the birds make of it –
the lack of noise and reverberation through the air ?
their world suddenly returned to the state of nature
their ancient memory recalls,
before the blip of human life intruded.
Will they breed more strongly in the clean air ?
Will the young ones chirp more freely ?
I watch the dawn light spreading
as they swoop and reform in clouds
of avian togetherness.
And I rejoice for them.

Section Six

Miscellaneous

Section Six

Miscellaneous

Prison – BT Style

Invisible bands close round
ever tighter
imprisoning our mental world.
'Press one, press two, press three.'
The electronic world rules.
'Hold for an advisor.'
Eventually a human voice
explains in rapid tones
a system so complex
my utmost concentration
barely understands.
We have imprisoned ourselves
in a virtual world
of non-sense.
Will there ever be a comeback
to a proper human exchange ?

Sleep, my sleep

That curtained deep
between one day's light
and another.
A proper separation allows
for each day's life
to begin afresh.
Not for me the hard night's work
of vivid dreams.
Only occasionally the helpmate
of Radio 3,
to anchor the subconscious mind
and allow the body sleep.
But the deep mind – to be refreshed
needs silence,
and out of the no man's land of sleep's forgetting
life rises, made anew in body, mind and soul.

Cpelling

In the abundance
of her teenage high-spiritedness,
what could the odd 'c' matter
in sircle, presipitate or presense ?
what to me is a fascinating link
with the past, threads
interwoven into a complex pattern,
reaching back into history
and literary heritage,
is to her a trap
for the unwary, deliberately
thought up to confuse!
And as for the verbs –
what's in a verb, when the description
is lively, imaginative, and full of
atmocphere – ah, there's the rub.
Where does this 'c' come ?
And will credit be given
by those fiends, the examiners,
for quality of thought,
or only for the exactitude
with which it is expressed ?

En

Encourage, enliven, enhance,
Enjoy, empower, endure –
That little symbol
that changes an impossible state of being
into an active possibility.

We have to summon our courage, yes,
when life is difficult,
but to be encouraged,
that sets us on our way.

Joy is a peak moment,
a shaft of light, catching us, unbidden, unawares.
But to enjoy – an act of will
set to an obtainable end.

Power may always elude us –
the sense of control over our lives or others,
but to be empowered
is to find the fulfilment of our potential.

We may not survive under duress
but 'Those who endure to the end
will be saved.'

A humble syllable,
tacked onto the forefront of strong nouns,
adding an enabling ingredient.

Music

Be like the camel.
Fill up your hump
not with material lump-
iness, but song –
Long for the music
that takes you to heaven.
Leaven life
not with strife
against the desert of worldliness.
But, be like the camel.
Fill up your hump
With sump –
tuous music –
And hold your head high
as you tread
threading your way
through the desert
singing, towards the last trump.

Bare knees

They sat side by side,
mother and handicapped son,
in shorts.

Bare knees reveal all –
Season, weather, physique –
even character, perhaps – and age.
The season of summer
when the bronzing torso revels
in the unrestricting air.
Sunny shedding of protective covering,
allowing penetrating warmth.
Physique – strong, sturdy.
Companionable knees, side by side,
telling of steady reliability,
the will to arrive, to achieve –
determinedly dependable –
the veined solidness of age
beside the pink freshness of knobbly youth.

Knees tell a story, a history,
when bared to the elements,
pleasured in the sunlight.

From a Hospital bed

Do not underestimate the humble biscuit.
A biscuit can settle the stomach
relieve the hungry mind
help induce sleep.
Do not underestimate the humble digestive.
Not half-baked but twice baked
in its effectiveness.

For Jane

I've heard of
tongue-tied
tongue twisters
and hold your tongue
But
cleaning your tongue
never.

I've heard of
to give tongue
learn a foreign tongue
and tonguing the recorder notes
for quickness
But
cleaning your tongue
never.

Perhaps if we all cleaned our tongues
we would untwist our thoughts
learn to express ourselves
in whatever language
with ease
and earn the right
to poke our tongues out
at whoever we please.

Section Seven

Reflections

Section Seven

Reflections

I wandered, lonely

I wandered, lonely,
in the solitude of self
that heals.
Not that I felt alone.
A cloud of witnesses hovered around
the edge of being – but did not intrude.

I, in my solitude, absorbed
the dappled sunlight on the autumn leaves,
the squirrel skittering off at heavy footfall,
the wind soughing in the swaying branches of oaks,
acorn laden.

Alone, but connected to all life that breathes,
gives praise.

This hour

How could I have better spent
this hour
in which I have done nothing
but sit by an open doorway
watching the rising millpond of a tide
slightly increase the distance
between the sunlit island and the shore.
Time has gone by,
but thought, emotion, has recalled the past,
and through the misty jumble of impressions
far-reaching and more recent
the rise of praise has, like a spider's thread
forever giving out its steel-strength web,
wound its intimate way through life's recall.

The tide has risen slightly.
An hour has passed.
Tranquility – of sun and sea has stayed
my outward eye –
and inwardly created calm.

In the shower

'I know God in the shower' she said
and we all laughed.
But I knew what she meant.
In a shower the mind is free flowing,
in touch with life, people one cares about, thoughts....
One meets God in the shower.

One meets God wherever the self is real,
in touch with life, circumstance, demands.
wherever the heart turns from cynicism
to trust –
and sometimes only worship will do that.

Intimacy

To be intimate
with another is a gift
that many people
long for.

To be intimate
with many others is a gift
some of us receive
in abundance.

To open oneself
to another's longing for intimacy
is to give a gift
unsurpassed.

It is a gift, the giving of which
we may all offer.

Grief

I used to think grief lasted two years –
one year to live through special occasions,
the second to let go.
But grief does not follow a straight path.
Grief ricochets about,
catching one off guard,
sometimes with pain,
other times with gratitude for what has been.

Association is strong,
often unexpected, triggered
by the chance remark,
the look alike person;
but sometimes constant
like the cup of tea, recalling
a mother's presence.

Love and friendship

In love is a fountain.
Friendship is a sparkling stream.
Love shoots high, shimmeringly,
then collapses in a splutter of small cascades.
Friendship bubbles along evenly,
surrounding stones, finding new paths, flexible.
Love's energy is a sprint, soon up and over.
Friendship is the long haul, constant, dependable.
Friendship wins.

Communion

We stood
by the kitchen sink,
in the quiet of the empty house
looking out at the garden, grown,
overgrown, but with a colourful display,
of flowers,
drinking our first coffee,
eating our first cake
in the new home.
Communion it was,
bread and wine for a new beginning.

Hope

I cry for the sorrow of the world
the sore, heaped up sadness
of tragedy and loss.
Let there be learning and love
to uplift the spirit,
the long, slow moulding of the soul
to – in the end – joy.

One experience

You only need one experience of loss
to understand how the world grieves.

You only need to see one war film
to understand the necessity of peace.

To experience once the pain of rejection
to understand the desperate need to belong.

One small experience creates
a larger understanding of the lot of humankind.

Being human

Include me in –
I'm a human being.
I may look odd,
seem on the edge of things,
don't talk easily,
but – include me in.
I'm a human being.

Include me in –
when you share your jokes –
and your laughter.
I may not seem to respond
but include me in –
I'm not used to it.

By a glance, a touch,
include me in.
I don't have to be the centre of attention,
but make room for me to be there –
part of your circle,
part of your friendly inclusion.

And don't be afraid to address me
because I am different.
I too have my thoughts and opinions
and long for the opportunity
to express them.
I would not be in need
if you gave me the chance
to be myself.

So include me in.
I'm a human being.
And never underestimate another human being.
One day, you may need me.

Be humble

Be humble
before your body.
It has a life of its own.
Only sometimes do you touch down
and link your will with its –
when you eat, drink, excrete,
and most intimately of all,
make love.
Be humble before your body.

So many of its functions happen
without your knowledge, let alone your will.
Hair grows, blood circulates, food digests,
few of us know how – and even if we knew
we could not control it.
The body has a mind of its own.

So do not push it too far.
Be sensitive to its rhythms,
respect its demands –
for rest, exercise, nourishment.
And when it lets you down,
as in illness or old-age
it surely will,
be gentle with it still.
It is a living growing organism,
generating its own healing powers,
and if we listen, it may dictate to us
what it needs. We,
with our superior knowledge,
can only help it along.

So be humble before your body.
It is the means of grace
in an incarnate world.
It is the expression of joy and well-being.
It deserves our respect,
and cooperation.

Twist of Love

The twist of light and dark
Runs through our earthly life.
Where shadows are the light is bright,
The darkness hides the seed.

The twist of good and ill
Runs through our earthly life.
Mistakes, confessions, sorrows, sins,
Bring fuller love to light.

The twist that Jesus brought
Runs through his earthly life,
That out of his self-giving love
God's purposes are wrought.

So let us now embrace
The paradox of life,
That God is in the good, the ill,
the light, The dark, the sin.

Give thanks a Greater Love
Runs through our earthly life,
That out of life's raw happenings
God twists his golden love.